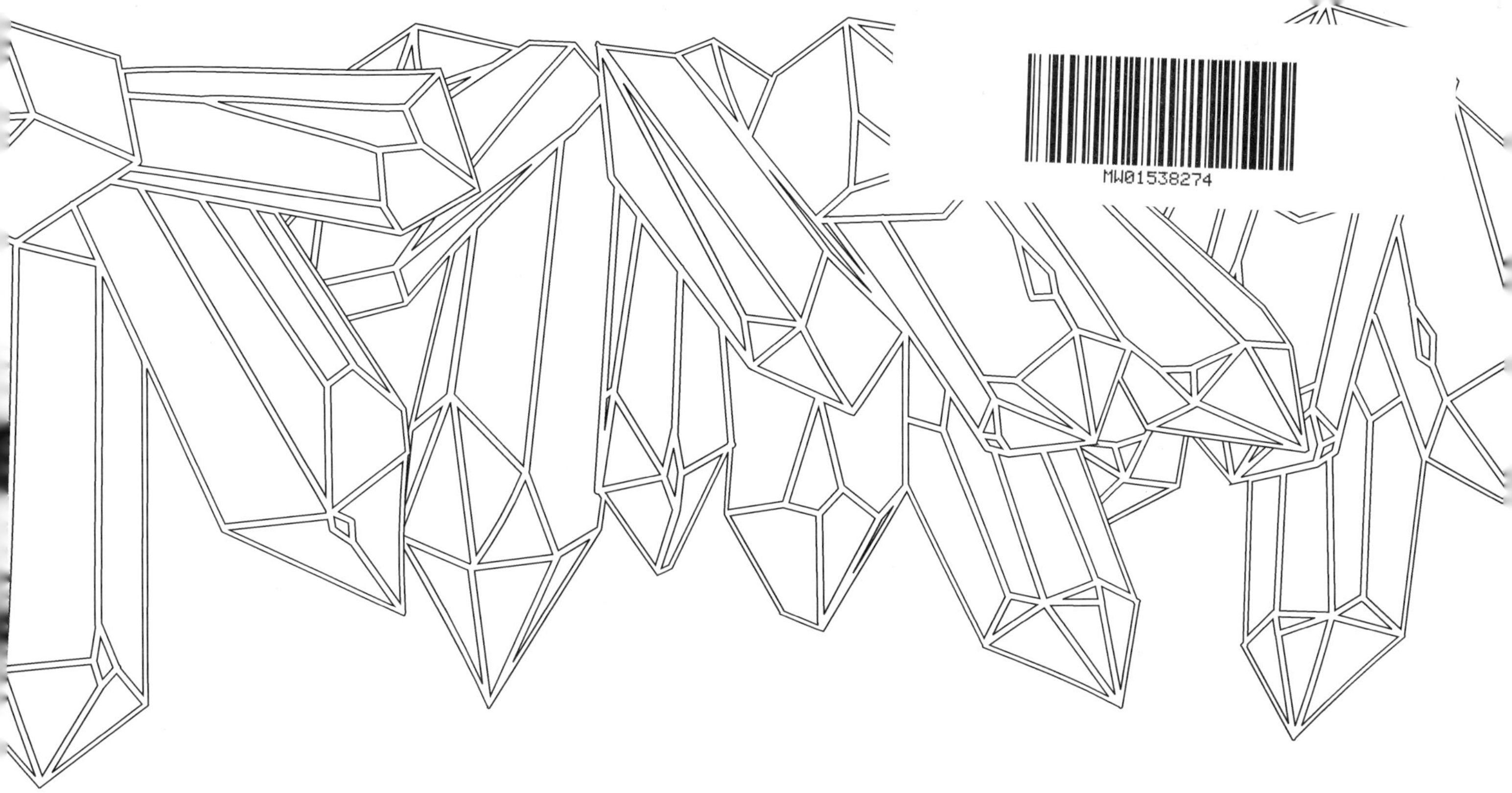

Positivity

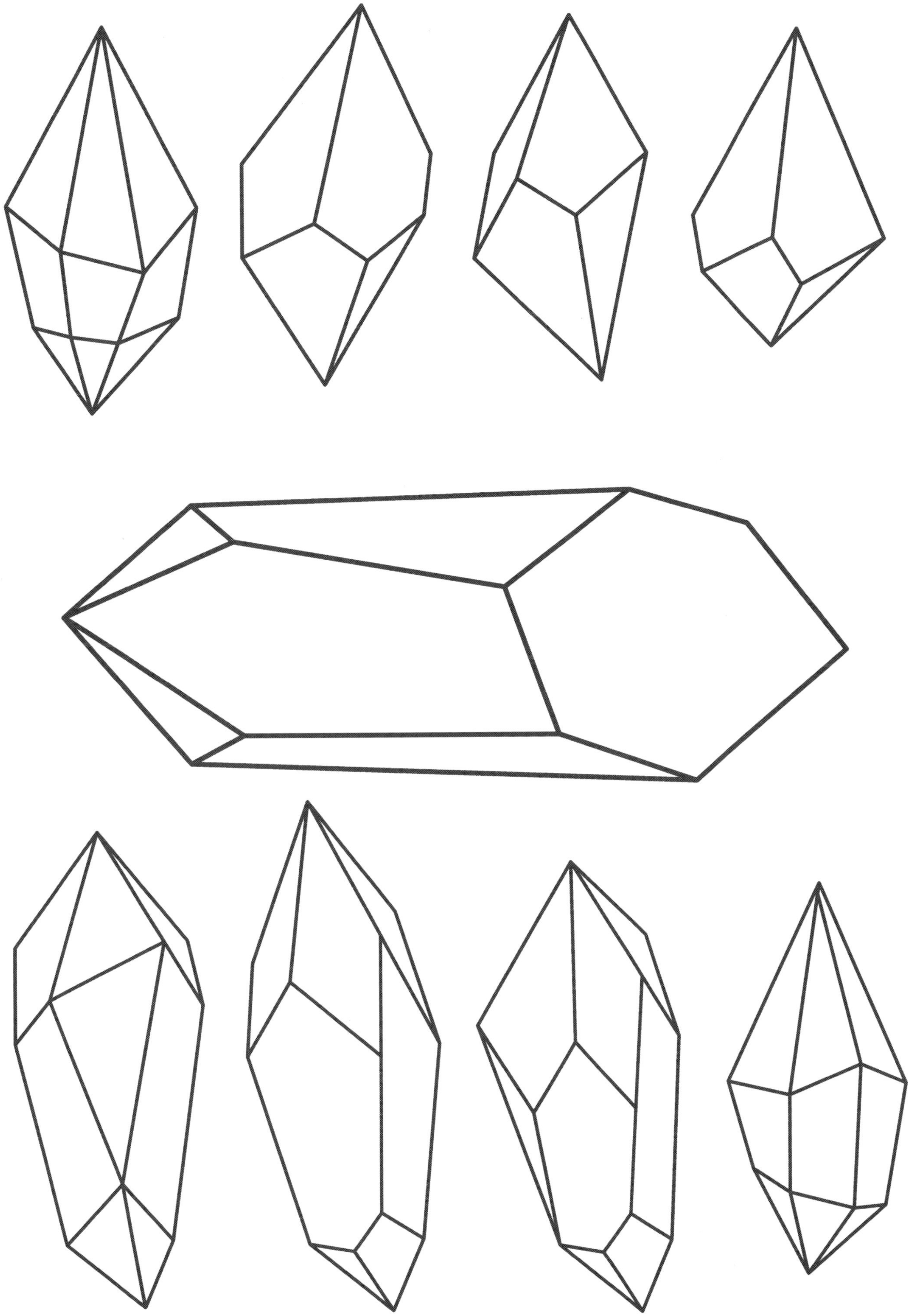

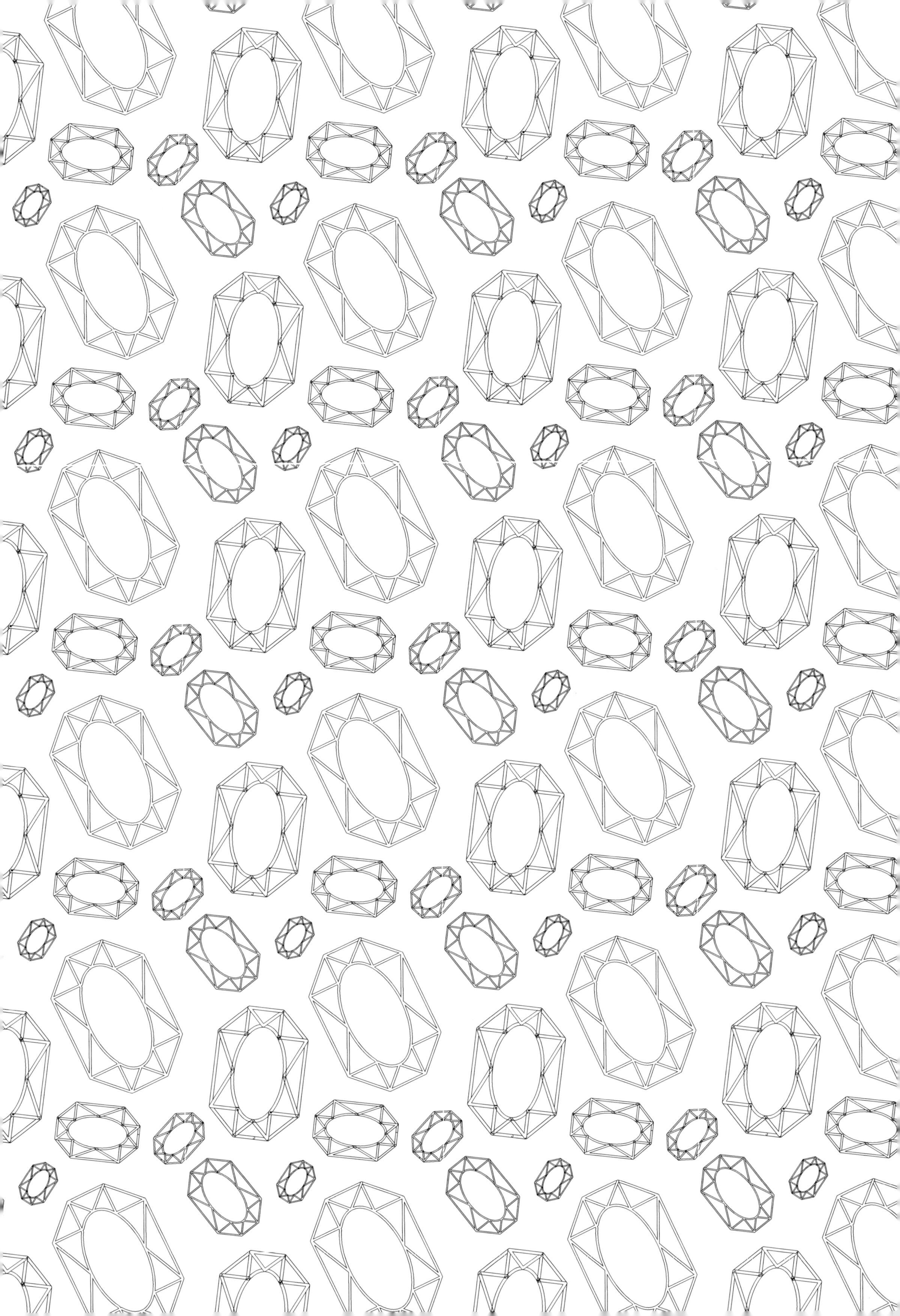

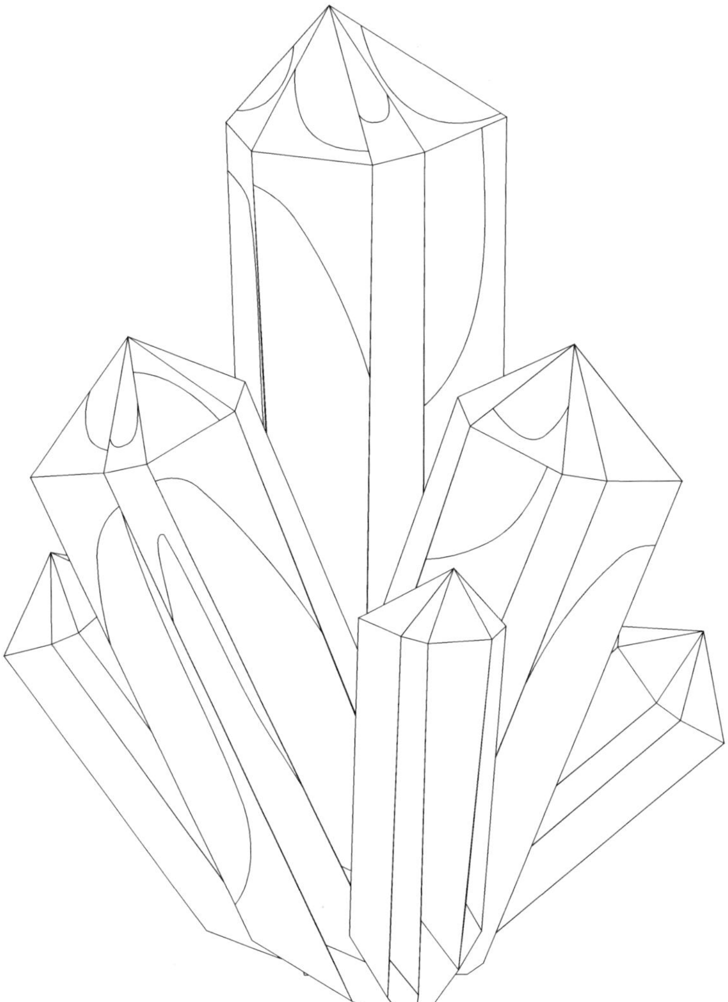
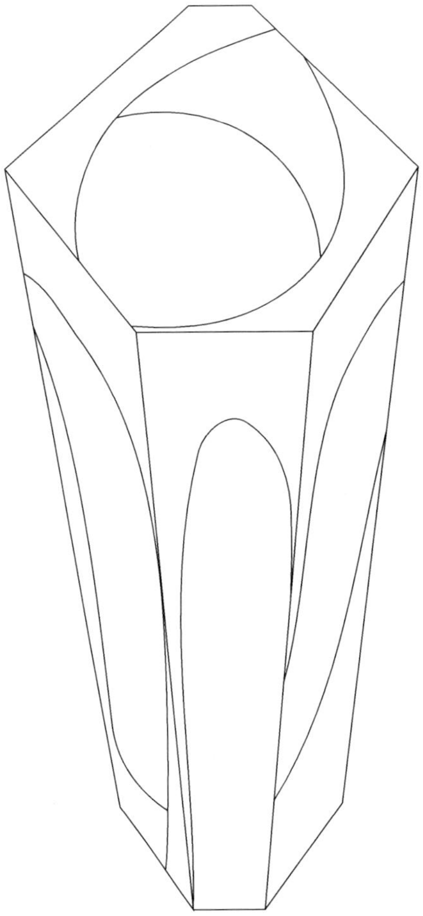

Magic

I

Crystals

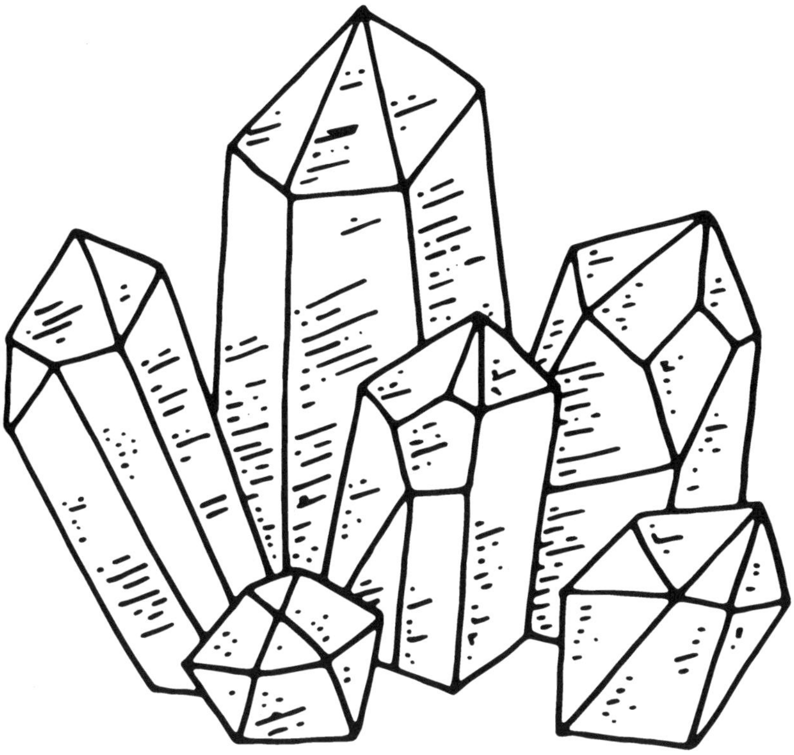

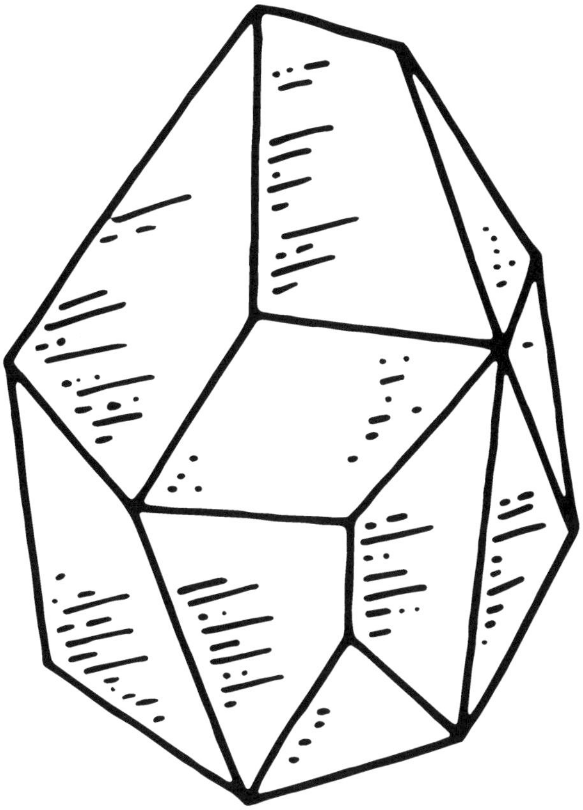

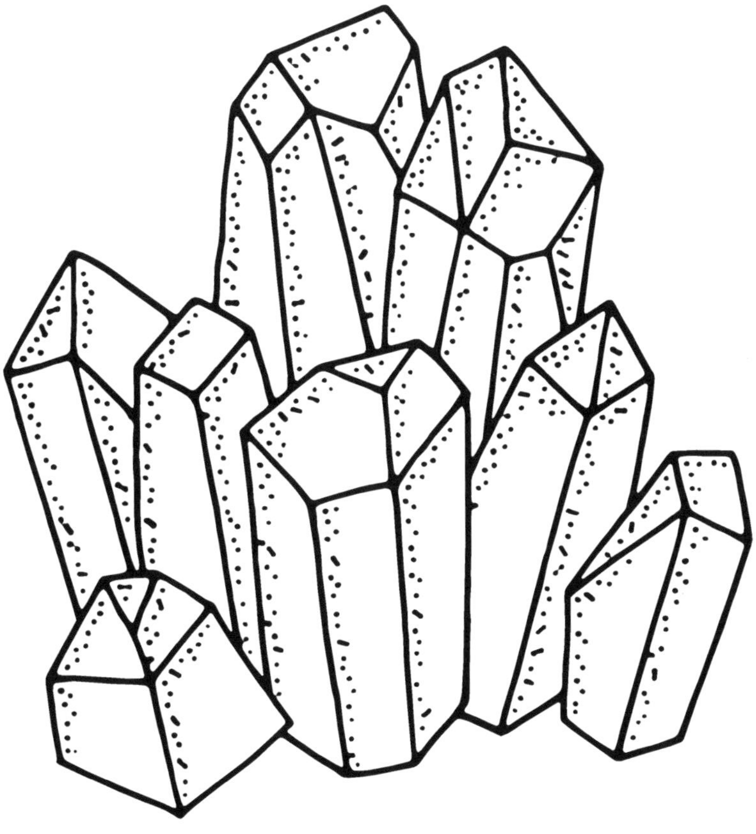

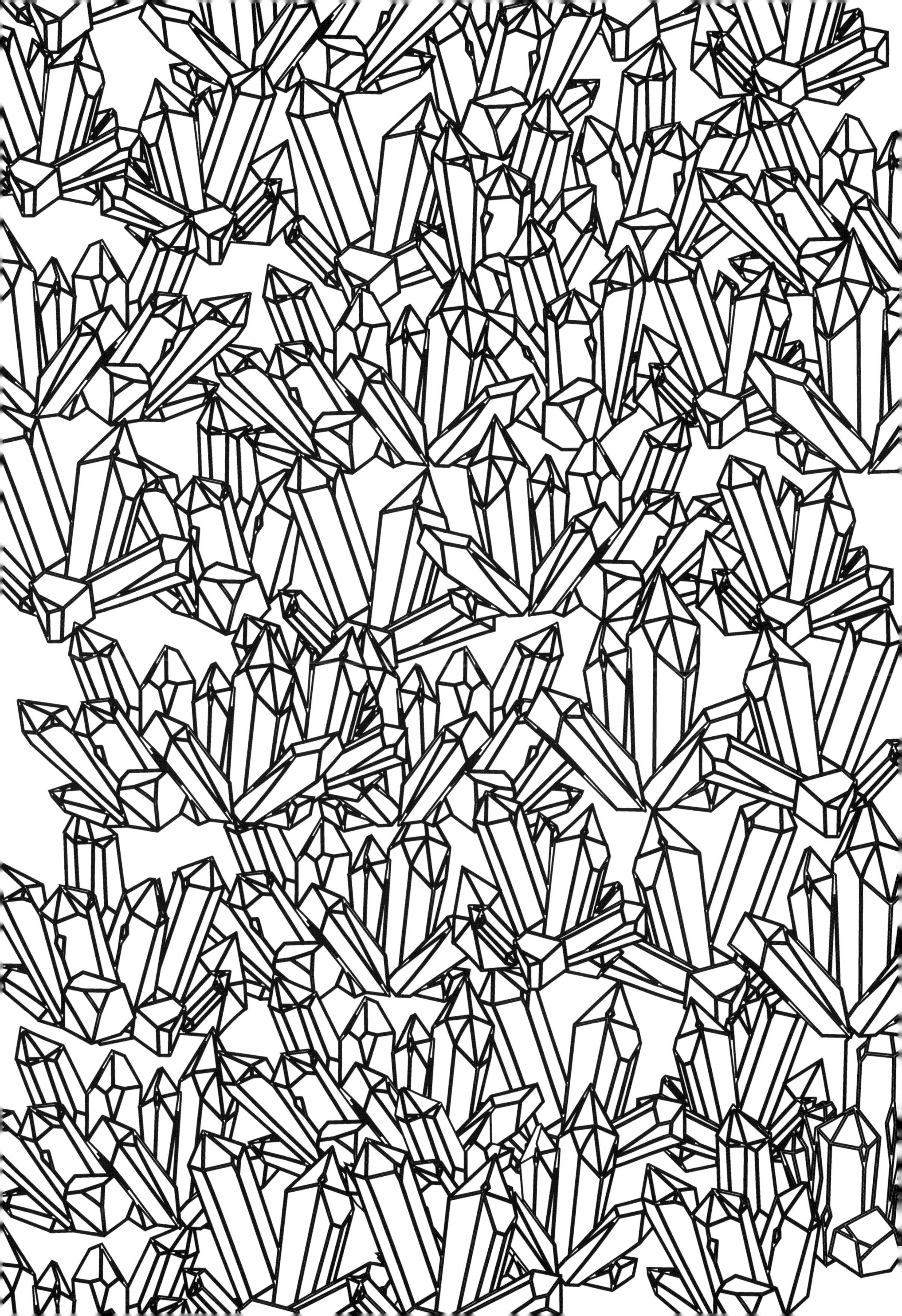

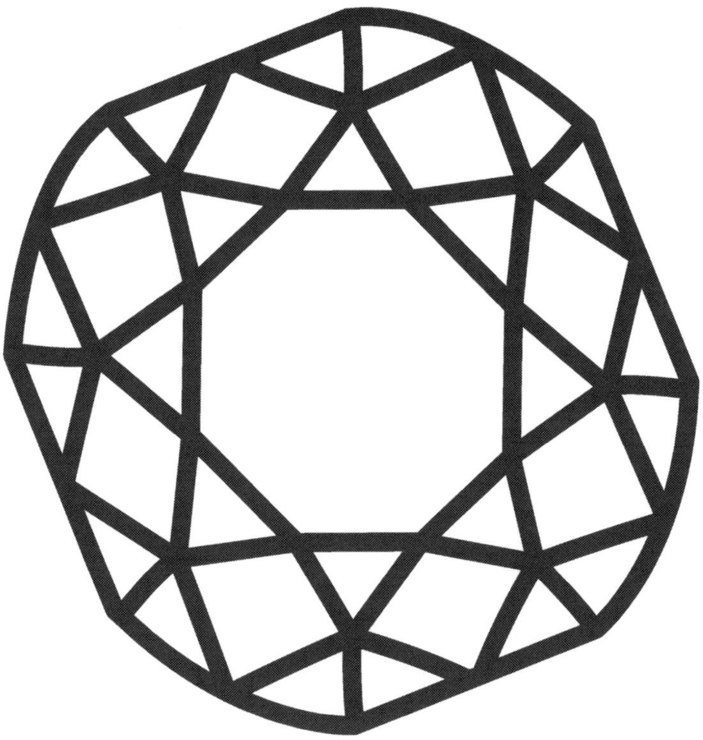
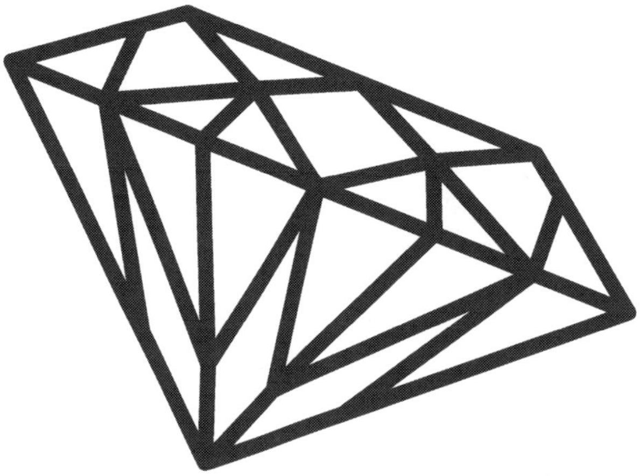

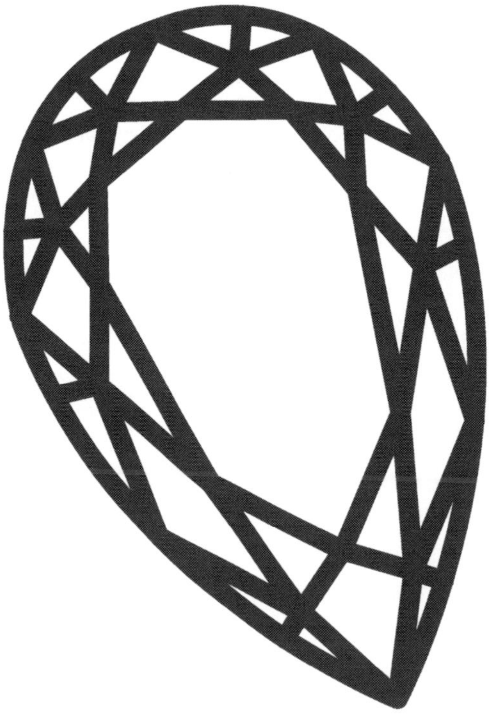
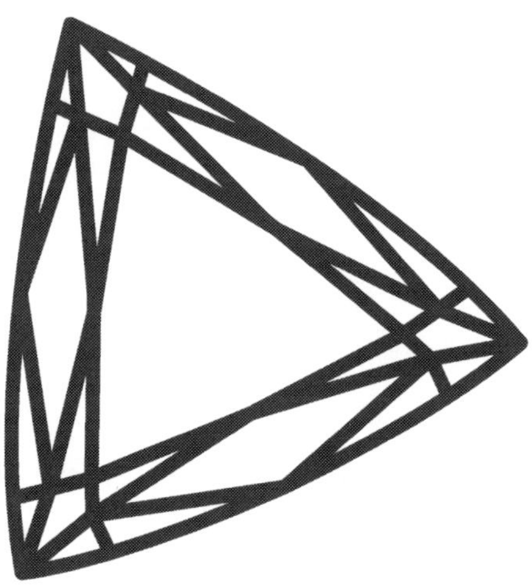

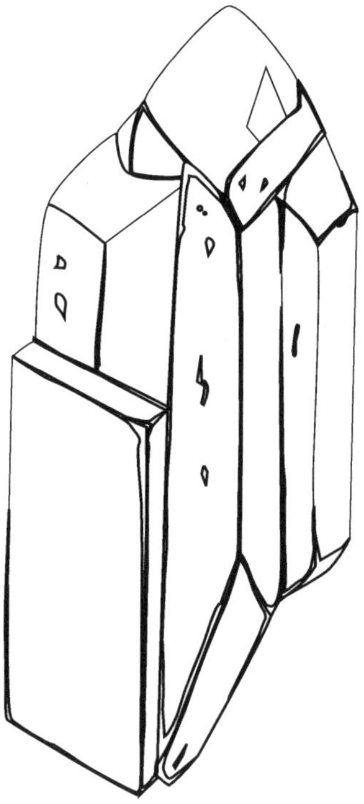

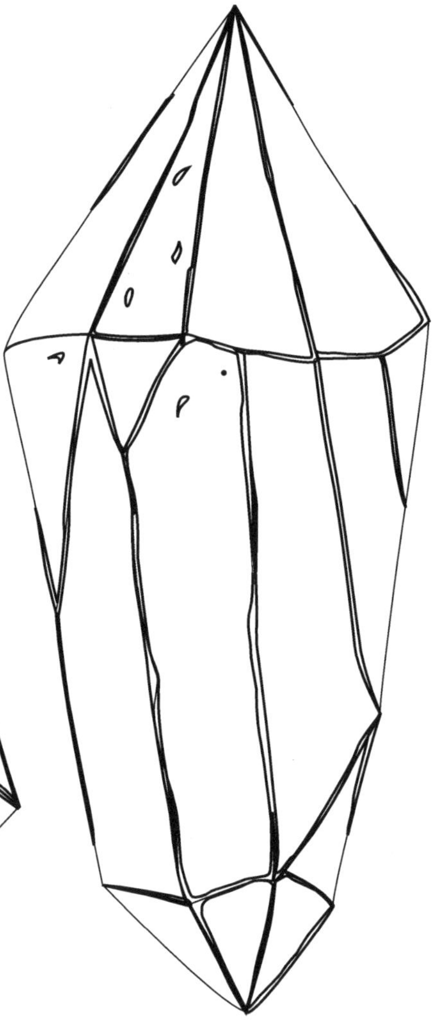
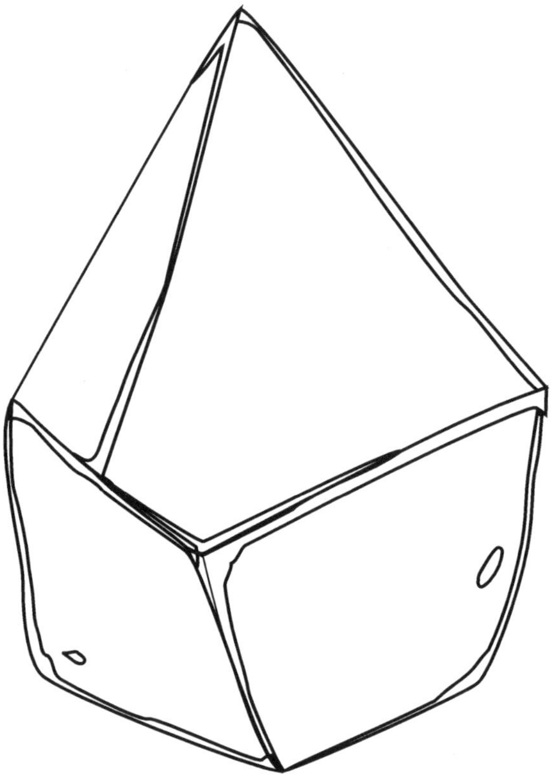
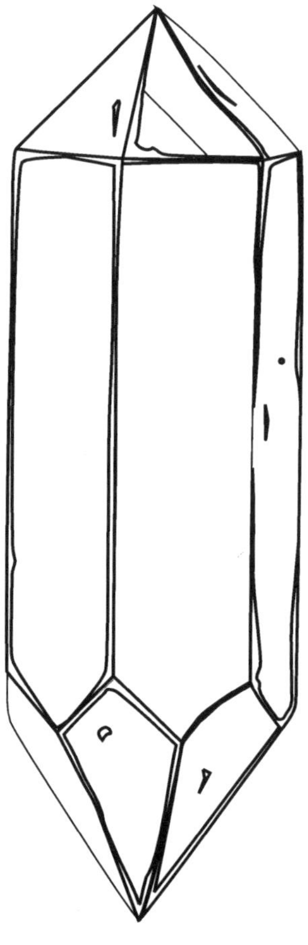
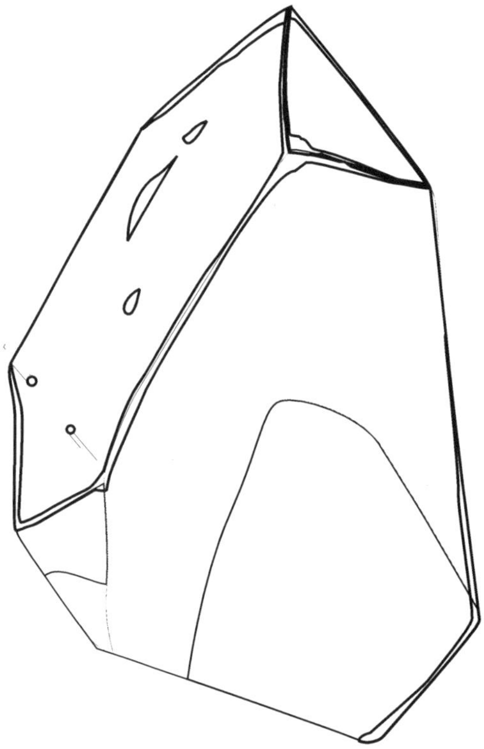

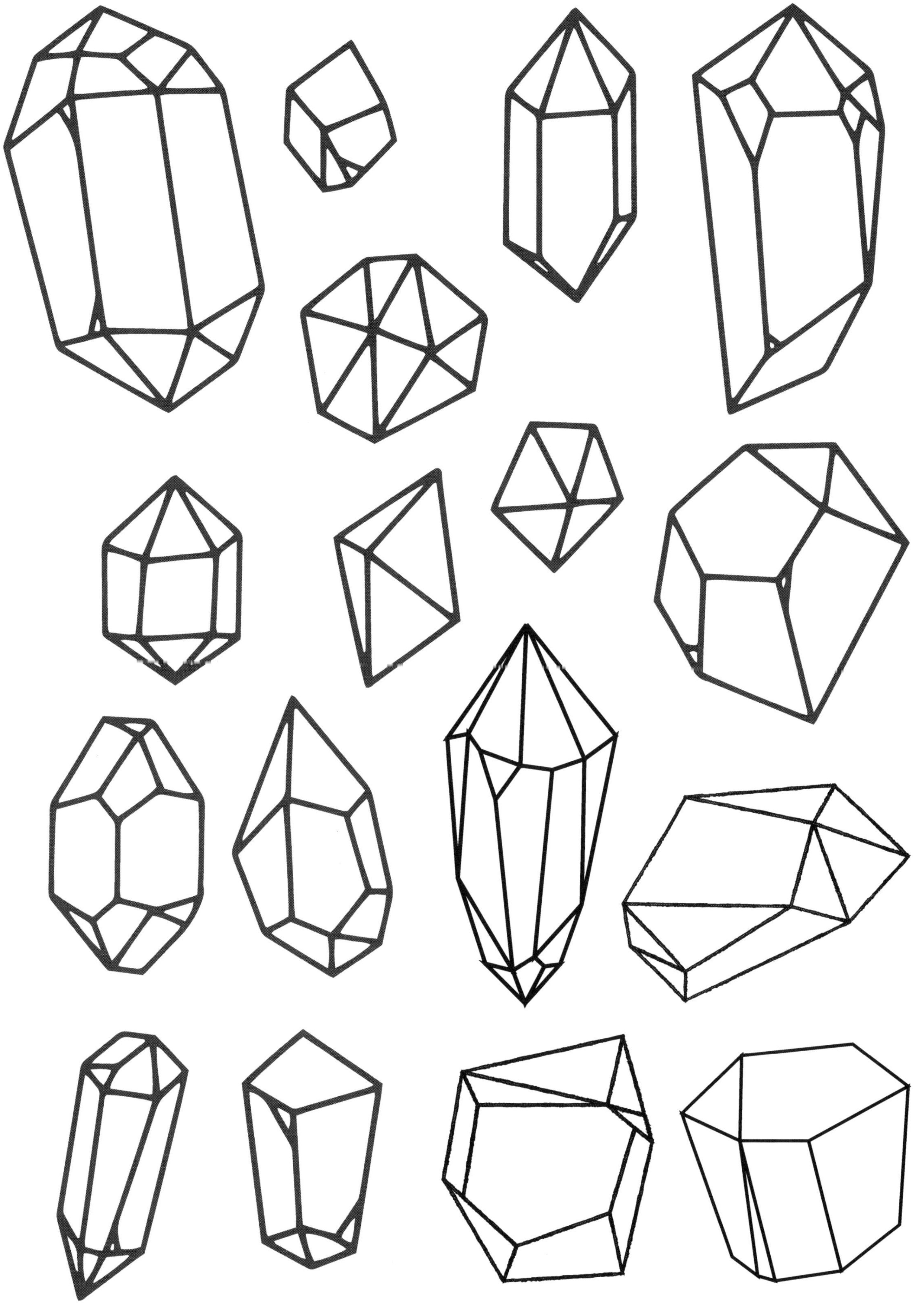

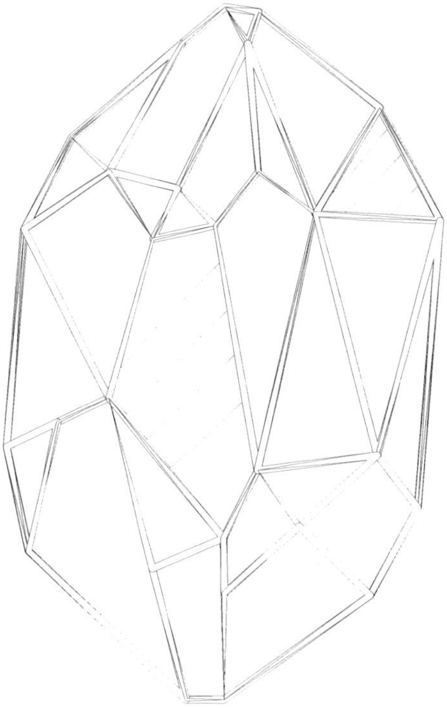

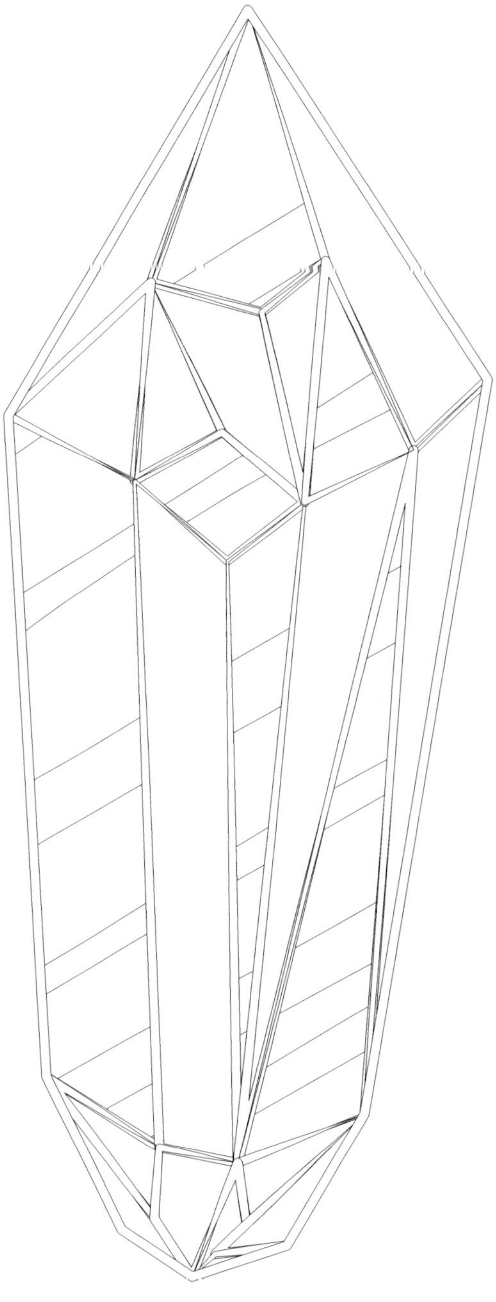

Precious

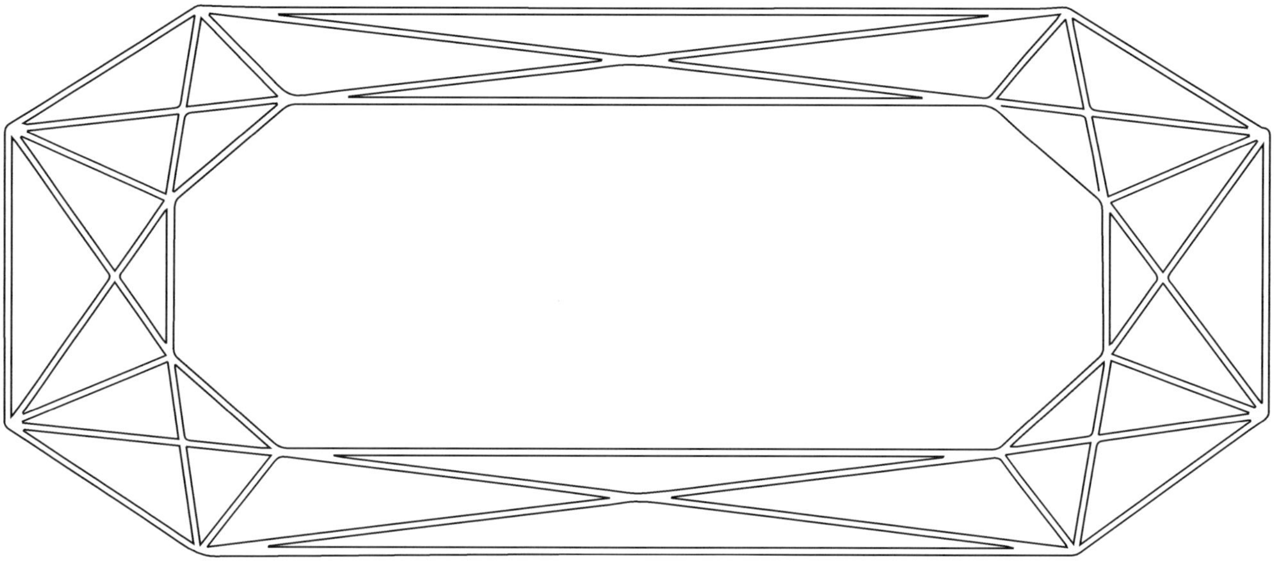

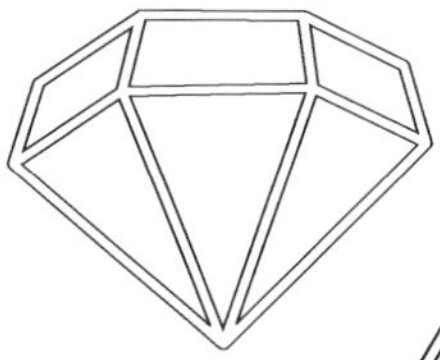

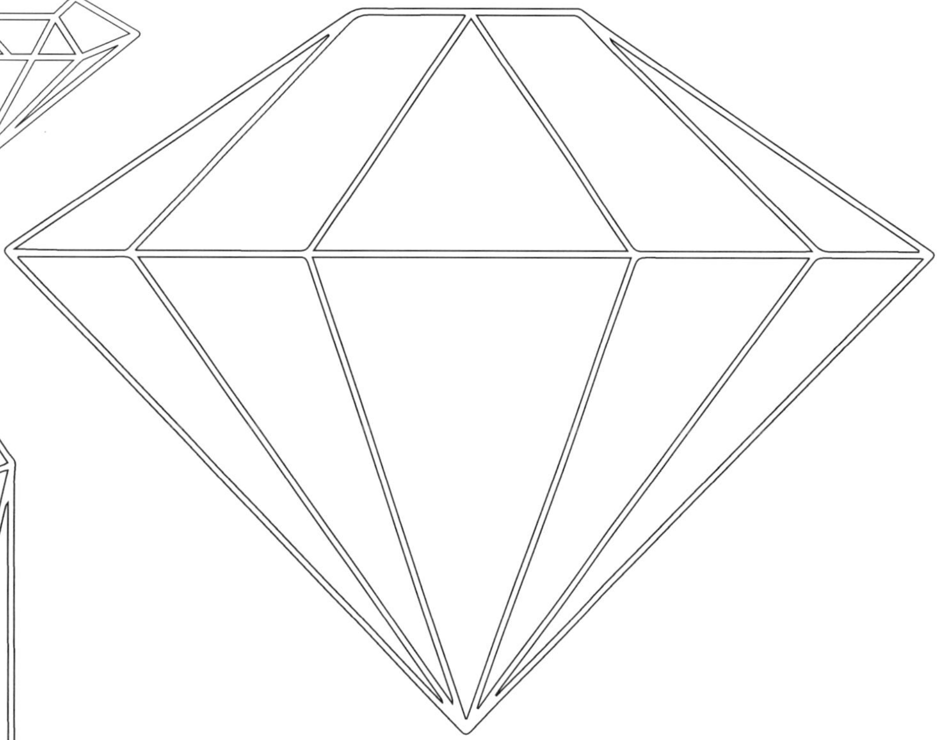

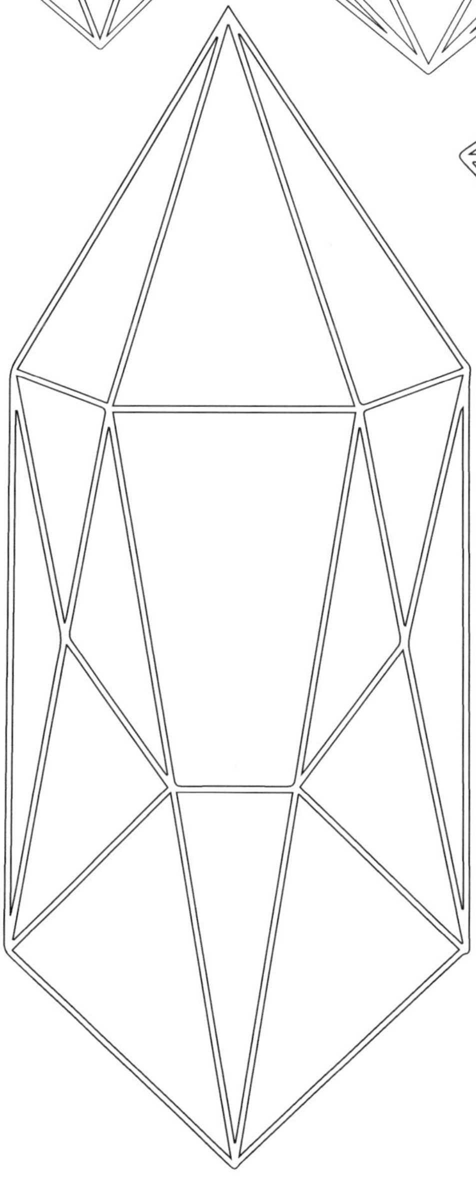

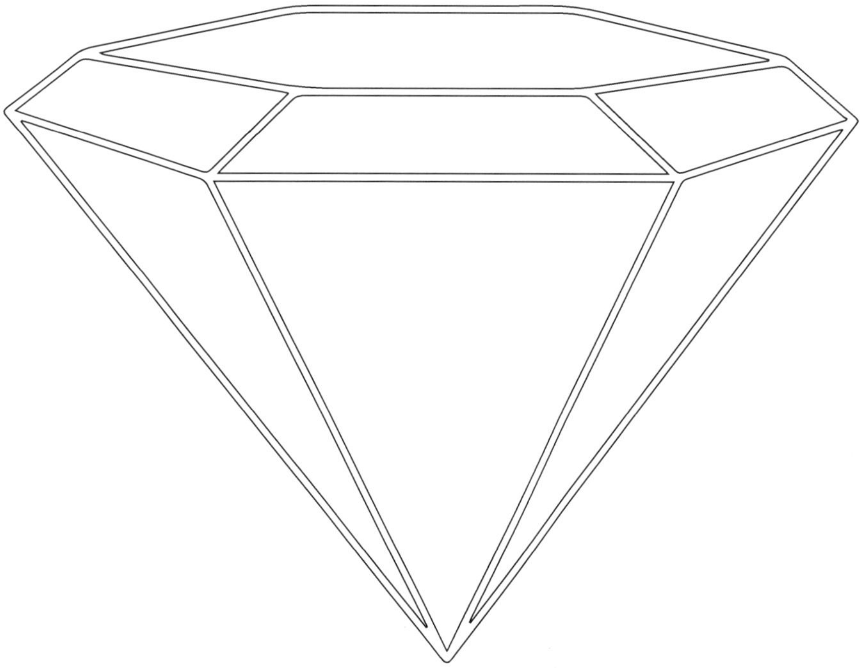

Made in United States
Troutdale, OR
02/17/2025